Your heart
will sing
again

First edition for the United States, its territories and possessions, and Canada published in 2010 by Barron's Educational Series, Inc.

All inquiries should be addressed to:
Barron's Educational Series, Inc.
250 Wireless Boulevard
Hauppauge, New York 11788
www.barronseduc.com

ISBN-13: 978-0-7641-6364-7
ISBN-10: 0-7641-6364-7

Library of Congress Control Number: 2010923665

First published in 2010 by
David Bateman Ltd.
30 Tarndale Grove
Albany
Auckland, New Zealand

Book design by Alice Bell

Printed in China through Colorcraft Ltd, Hong Kong

9 8 7 6 5 4 3 2 1

Your heart will sing again

COMFORT FOR THOSE WHO MOURN

Gillian and Darryl Torckler

BARRON'S

When you are sorrowful
look again in your heart,
and you shall see that in truth
you are weeping for that
which has been your delight.

Kahlil Gibran

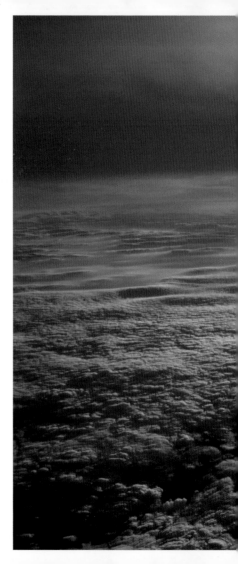

Grief is normal.
Grief will pass.
Grief will hurt.
Grief will teach.

Grief is love.

Death hurts.

To love a thing means
wanting it to live.

Confucius

It fills you with memories,

fills you with regret,

*and fills your
eyes with tears.*

The soul would have no rainbow
had the eyes no tears.

John Vance Cheney

What comes from the heart,
goes to the heart.

Samuel Taylor Coleridge

Death makes you angry,

Anger is one of the sinews of the soul.

Thomas Fuller

confuses you,

and makes you sad.

Sadness flies away on the wings of time.

Jean de La Fontaine

Grief is an uninvited visitor,

reluctant to leave,

that finds you unprepared

*and overwhelms
everything.*

When it is dark enough,
you can see the stars.

Ralph Waldo Emerson

Grief feels like guilt;
like fear;
like illness.

Pain and death are part of life.
To reject them is to reject life itself.

Havelock Ellis

Grief needs company,

and seeks solace.

Grief ebbs and flows.

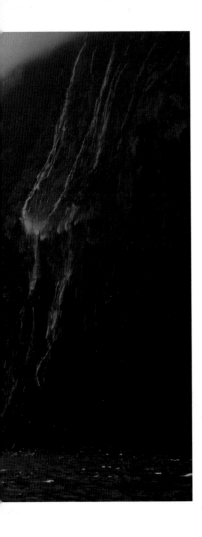

There will be good days; bad days; and difficult days.

Into each life some rain must fall.

Henry Wadsworth Longfellow

Grief is love.

While we are mourning the loss of our friend,
others are rejoicing to meet him behind the veil.

John Taylor

With time,
grief's force
will diminish.

Time is a physician that heals every grief.

Diphilius

freedom will return:

freedom to be happy;

The sweetness that comes after grief,
you will find after you have gone through grief.

Aldo Kraas

freedom to remember;

Remember me when I am gone away,
Gone far away into the silent land.

Christina Rossetti

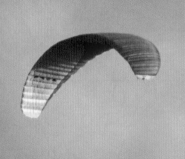

freedom to live;

I have woven a parachute out of
everything broken.

William Stafford

and freedom to love.

Too long the sacrifice,
can make a stone of the heart.

W. B. Yeats

Your head will stop seeking explanations,

and your pain will recede.

However long the night, the dawn will break.

African Proverb

Your heart will be scarred,

What deep wounds ever closed without a scar?

Lord Byron

*but your heart
will sing again:*

not the same song,

not a weaker song,

just a different song.

Death leaves a heartache no one can heal,
love leaves a memory no one can steal.

Anon